J597
12.95

THE WORLD'S BIGGEST

FISH

by Mari Schuh

Ideas for Parents and Teachers

Pogo Books let children practice reading informational text while introducing them to nonfiction features such as headings, labels, sidebars, maps, and diagrams, as well as a table of contents, glossary, and index.

Carefully leveled text with a strong photo match offers early fluent readers the support they need to succeed.

Before Reading

- "Walk" through the book and point out the various nonfiction features. Ask the student what purpose each feature serves.
- Look at the glossary together. Read and discuss the words.

Read the Book

- Have the child read the book independently.
- Invite him or her to list questions that arise from reading.

After Reading

- Discuss the child's questions. Talk about how he or she might find answers to those questions.
- Prompt the child to think more. Ask: What is the biggest fish you have ever seen?

Pogo Books are published by Jump!
5357 Penn Avenue South
Minneapolis, MN 55419
www.jumplibrary.com

Library of Congress Cataloging-in-Publication Data

Schuh, Mari C., 1975- author.
  The world's biggest fish / by Mari Schuh.
      pages cm. – (The world's biggest animals)
  "Pogo Books are published by Jump!."
  Audience: Ages 7-10
  Includes index.
  ISBN 978-1-62031-207-0 (hardcover: alk. paper) –
  ISBN 978-1-62031-262-9 (paperback) –
  ISBN 978-1-62496-294-3 (ebook)
  1. Fishes—Size—Juvenile literature.
  2. Whale shark—Juvenile literature.
  3. Ocean sunfish—Juvenile literature. I. Title.
  QL617.2.S375 2016
  597—dc23
                                                 2014049511

Series Editor: Jenny Fretland VanVoorst
Series Designer: Anna Peterson
Photo Researcher: Anna Peterson

Photo Credits: Alamy, 3, 8-9; Getty, 16-17; iStock, 1; Shutterstock, 1, 4, 5, 23; SuperStock, cover, 6, 7, 10-11, 12-13, 14, 15, 18-19, 20-21.

Printed in the United States of America at Corporate Graphics in North Mankato, Minnesota.

TABLE OF CONTENTS

CHAPTER 1

WHAT ARE FISH?

A trout swims in a shallow stream.

A stingray finds food on the **ocean** floor.

What do these animals have in common?

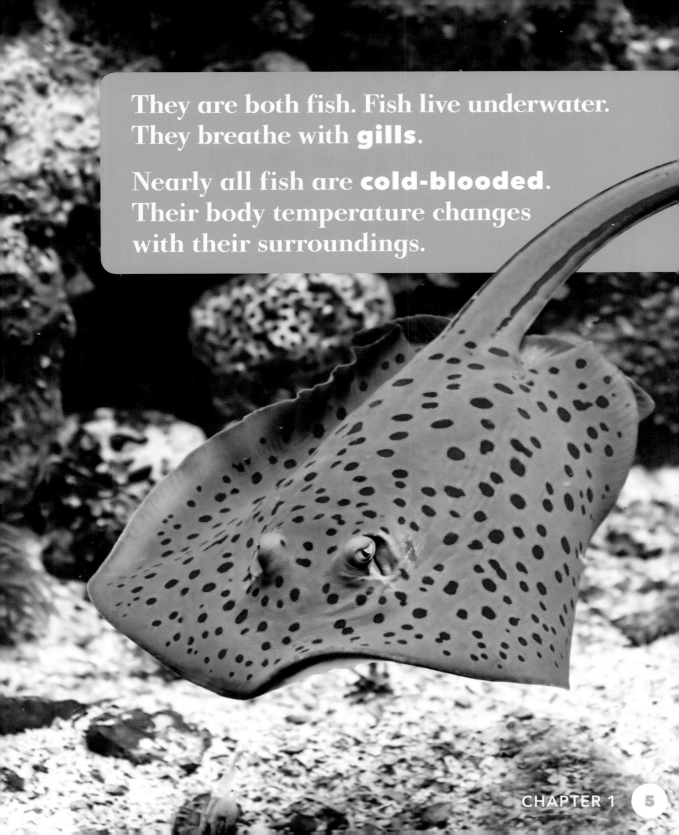

They are both fish. Fish live underwater. They breathe with **gills**.

Nearly all fish are **cold-blooded**. Their body temperature changes with their surroundings.

CHAPTER 2

JUMBO FISH

Ocean sunfish are the heaviest bony fish in the world.

These funny-looking fish can weigh up to 5,000 pounds (2,268 kilograms).

That's more than a minivan!

Unlike most fish, ocean sunfish don't have a tail fin. But they are still huge fish.

They can grow about 10 feet (3 meters) long. That is as long as a small room!

Ocean sunfish are also very tall. They can be 14 feet (4.3 m) from the top fin to the bottom. That is taller than an adult human!

DID YOU KNOW?

Ocean sunfish have huge fins on the top and bottom of their body.

When they swim close to the surface, their top fin sticks out of the water. It looks like a shark fin!

14 feet
(3 m)

5½ feet
(1⅔ m)

Ocean sunfish have small mouths.

But that doesn't stop them from eating lots of **prey**.

Ocean sunfish eat mostly jellyfish.

They also eat **algae** and small fish.

DID YOU KNOW?

Some fish like the ocean sunfish have bones. Other fish, like whale sharks, have **cartilage**. Cartilage is tough and flexible.

Some animals have both bones and cartilage. Like you!

jellyfish

mouth

algae

WHERE ARE THEY?

Ocean sunfish live in oceans around the world.
They swim in mild and warm water.

Adult ocean sunfish usually swim alone.
They **migrate** long distances to look for food.

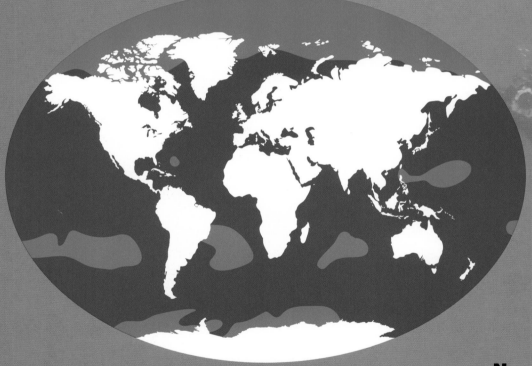

■ = Ocean Sunfish Range

Ocean sunfish are the biggest bony fish, but they aren't the biggest fish in the world.

It takes six heavy ocean sunfish to weigh as much as one whale shark.

CHAPTER 3

· ·

GIANT SHARKS

Whale sharks are the
biggest fish in the world.

Some weigh more than 30,000 pounds (13,608 kg).

That is more than eight cars!

Whale sharks are not whales. They are sharks, a kind of fish.

Whale sharks can be about 40 feet (12 m) long. That's about the length of a school bus!

DID YOU KNOW?

Female whale sharks make eggs. Each egg is as big as a football.

Pups hatch from the eggs while they are still inside their mother's body. Then she gives birth to the pups.

A whale shark has a flat head and a wide mouth. The mouth can be four feet (1.2 m) wide.

It holds about 300 rows of tiny teeth! But whale sharks do not use their teeth to eat.

Instead, whale sharks swim with their mouth open. They suck in water, **plankton**, and small fish.

Whale sharks trap the food in their mouth. Then the water flows out their gills.

WHERE ARE THEY?

Whale sharks live in oceans around the world. They swim in warm water near the **equator**.

Whale sharks usually swim alone. Sometimes they eat together in groups.

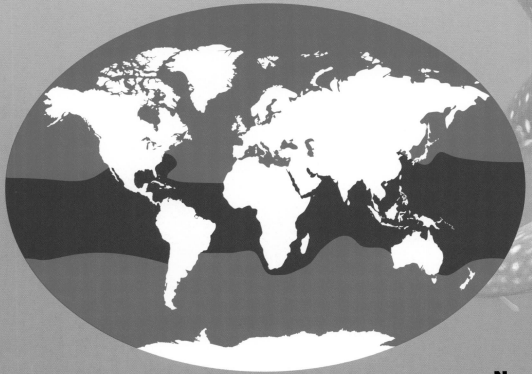

■ = Whale Shark Range

Giant whale sharks gulp up food with their big mouths. Huge ocean sunfish swim slowly through the sea.

What is the biggest fish you have ever seen?

ACTIVITIES & TOOLS

A whale shark can weigh as much as six ocean sunfish.
An ocean sunfish can weigh as much as 100 second graders!

TRY THIS!

Whale sharks have 300 rows of tiny teeth. How many teeth do you have? Look in a mirror and open your mouth. Have an adult help you count.

. . . .

GLOSSARY

algae: Small plants without roots that grow in water or on damp surfaces.

cartilage: A strong, bendy type of tissue.

cold-blooded: Having a body temperature that changes with the surroundings.

equator: An imaginary line around the middle of Earth.

gills: A body part on the side of a fish; fish use their gills to breathe.

migrate: To move regularly from one place to another.

ocean: A large body of salt water.

plankton: Very tiny plants and animals that float in the ocean.

prey: Insects and animals that are hunted for food.

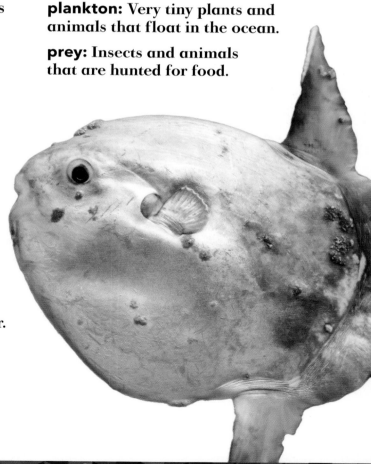

INDEX

TO LEARN MORE

Learning more is as easy as 1, 2, 3.

1) Go to www.factsurfer.com

2) Enter "biggestfish" into the search box.

3) Click the "Surf" to see a list of websites.

With factsurfer, finding more information is just a click away.